Love

Songs

on a

Mixtape

Love Songs on a Mixtape

Love Songs on a Mixtape

Emeka Barclay

Love Songs on a Mixtape

DEDICATION

words that create fire
and wings that give flight

to the one who will catch my breath
and hold my heart

Love Songs on a Mixtape

ACKNOWLEDGMENTS

Thank you to every soul and heart that has
blessed me
with an ear,
words of inspiration,
words of motivation,
honesty,
truth,
humor,
and surprise.

And a special thanks to the lovers who
journey here. I hope you find a moment
and remember along.

Love Songs on a Mixtape

Contents

Love Songs on a Mixtape

Love Songs on a Mixtape

Gravity and Light

I love you like the first time
again
and then time is forgotten
love with the strength
of Jupiterian gravity
and then
the withdrawal pains
that make me replay
the amazings

I am not ashamed to say
the things that have changed
are the very things that make
me love you more
as the one friend
the gravity and light

I lost myself for you
and you found me
presented the real me to myself as if
I was the queen of
the world
and reminded me of my greatness
and to
never settle

Mixtape

I remember the love songs on the first
mixtape given to me
thinking he was crazy
too familiar to be so foolish
too young to be interested
or me be interesting
with my
glasses, braces, bushy unprocessed hair,
nose in books
lost for days

I remember attaching to my Walkman for
the weekend
batteries dying while I slept
confused by his intentions
amazed at the thoughtfulness
the care given to what
he wanted to tell
me

I remember losing myself in the music
to that feeling that makes you
smile at walls and peer out windows
like Disney princesses
feelings new to me
liking a boy more than the flirting and
passing notes
that innocents do

Love Songs on a Mixtape

I remember desperately wanting to feel
it would have been the perfect young love
on which diamond anniversaries are
built
but I can only remember those love songs
on a mixtape
and my discovered love
of another

Love Songs on a Mixtape

Kiss

We hold hands and clutch
tight with our fingers sweaty and
white-tipped
in the delicious fear of being caught
at first love's kiss

that risk of wanting a taste of my
cherry-glossed lips
draws you in closer
and my heart races
not only
at the warm smell of your skin
and not because
soon people will begin to pass our corner
possibly wanting their few moments alone
risking love's kiss
but because I am ready to test my
technique
(practiced on the soft side of my fisted
hand)

I think you hesitate in want of
someone seeing you steal
the sweetness from me
pride in young love is tempting
but the silver-braced smile
and the sweet smell of my cherry lip-gloss
are too much for you

4

Love Songs on a Mixtape

and you lean in
and kiss me
with the swiftness
of a moment turned memory
and the risk becomes
the worth
of a first kiss

Flowing Like Milk and Honey

Words don't escape me
I let them out silky
and smooth like warm honey
that erupts from my fingertips
and I take a lick
enjoying the sweetness of my
thoughts.

But when the words escape me
I let them linger
and spin like fresh cream
to puddles on the page
and I dip my fingertips
in for a taste.

My words flow like
milk and honey
in a land of plenty and still
there is never enough
of the pleasures given
to the paper that catches
the sweetness of
the words I taste.

That Song

Long before the melody,
I was the bass line
Long before the rhythm
I was the beat
All the way back to the notes you sang
the chorus you wrote
It was me
I was the song
you couldn't finish writing
so you
put me on a demo tape
and gave me away
now someone else sings
and I will forever be
their
greatest hit

Love Me, A Resume

Do you have what it takes to love me?

I talk fast and say way more than what I
mean
but if you listen
you will hear the insecurity in the
intelligence
and the cocky badass breaking free

I laugh out loud and not always when it is
appropriate
a loud laugh that startles and confuses the
crowd
it is not cute, but it could be
if you have what it takes to love me.

I fall in love with the simplest of things
and my favorites are fleeting
a spoon that stirred the tea that I drank as
I watched something that made me feel a
particular way

I will love that spoon even if I can't tell
it from the other nine identical ones in the
drawer

I anticipate
and procrastinate

Love Songs on a Mixtape

I sleep in t-shirts or not
and I don't have a bedtime or I go to bed
early
and do not think I am a morning person
unless you wake up to the insatiable me
wanting a sleepy you because
you have what it takes to love me

I am playful, an insufferable flirt full of
infectious smiles that will light your life
but when the storm comes
I have days as dark as a moonless winter
night

I am strong, a tornadic force fueled by
caffeine and euphoria
and then I become the one who needs and
wants to be held and cherished and
supported and pushed and praised for the
amazing woman that I am
for the one that has what it takes to love
me.

In between

Time stands still
in the in-between
between the times that we know
won't last forever
and still without knowing when
we find ourselves right back
at the beginning of our time
and we cherish every moment
never knowing when the last
will be
but always knowing that
time stands still
for us

Waterdance

From trickles, a stream
quietly flows sweetly through as
water meets water in dance

Love Songs on a Mixtape

And I Fell in Love

I remember the first time I fell
in love
No dreamy montage of fairy tale castles
Backlit by the glow of happily-ever afters
No costumed animals singing a love song
Just the anti-climatic bubble bursting of
my realization
an explosion
So frightening and sudden.

He simply asked me for a kiss.

"May I kiss you?" from soft ample lips
so close to my face that I could feel the
warmth of his breath
Tickling skin

Me, breathing him in
eagerly anticipating
Then and there, in the silence of the night,
my skin screamed,
my heart pounded,
my stomach fluttered
for a kiss

gently and hungrily
pulling the filament and ether
so suddenly from me

Love Songs on a Mixtape

that I didn't feel it as it escaped
in tiny flutters of a breathtaking
heartbeat

the kiss stole my heart
and I fell in love

not wanting
to
not needing
to
but willing
to
again and again and again

Love Songs on a Mixtape

Waay Back

Waay back to middle school
summer weekends at the ballfield
and those busy signals of the
party lines
you call him and them
I'll call my girls
seven to eleven
phones connected
night hours
people trying to be heard at the same time
babysitting
phonesitting
conversations that I can't remember
but good times I can't forget
friends and friends of friends
courting and laughing
and passing notes
long before cell phones and texts
Facebook and Snapchat
Messenger and videos
way back before we cared
that time doesn't stand
still

All the World

If I could give you the world
I would love you
all the world

          is me.

If I could make you my everything
I would love you
everything

          is me.

If I could be yours
I would love you
all of you

          is me.

But,
I can't
give you the world

          love you
make you my everything

          love you
be yours

          love you
even though I want nothing more than
all the world
everything, all of you,
isn't enough

          for me.

Too Much

Love gives away too much fleetingly
and I shouldn't lose
to someone who can't cherish me
but, that night

filament and ether

words on wings

a kiss became a conversation
a conversation became moments
and I unexpectedly lost my heart and my
mind
in moments that lasted a lifetime

Last Poet

I have fallen in love with the
last poet
I heard him speak
through words so sweet
they stuck to me
in an audible residue
that can be heard
with each breath
that I take
and though I know
the infidelity
of his words
how they speak to each of you
touching you intimately
finding that spot
I know that his words
and I alone
share a connection
so profound
that he only exists
because I thought
he could be that
sound

Petals

Petals open as
the soft flower blooms in heat
releasing sweetness

Font

I miss you
in the smallest font
possible
because when I loved you
large and bold
you folded the page
and kept me in the pocket
that collects
hearts like a junk drawer
I don't miss you on paper
I miss you in the words spoken
that will come and go unless
I small font say it
to the click of an unlocked screen
and very soft keys

Becomes Forgotten

The last time I cried
I cried for you
cried in a love so consuming that
the ability to breath
became a second thought
I have loved
so hard that even
God has struggled to tear me away
and just when I find myself
slowing in orbit
You shine your light
and reveal your love
and breathe becomes
forgotten
again

Curse

Love is never equal between lovers
that is the curse
that keeps one pulling
and tugging
and breaking
the other clinging to what
was once shared
felt and needed
but lovers grow
and outgrow each other
because we never intended to grow
together
Different roots cursed
grounds
different blooms cursed
stems
We are lovers cursed to
love

Love Songs on a Mixtape

Knowing Never

Ever wonder where you'd be
if I'd let you get to know me?
No,
not the parts that you want to touch
or that catch your eye
or that linger long after I leave
Know
the real me
the one who smiles because everyone is
looking or
expecting me to glow
the one who loves hearts
more than books
and the one who
would have loved
you
knowing me.

Ever wonder where I'd be
if you'd let me get to know you?
The parts that I wanted to touch
the looks that caught my eye
the thoughts that linger long after you left.
The real you
that made me smile because
you were looking and expecting me to
the one who protects hearts
more than dreams

22

Love Songs on a Mixtape

and the one who
would have loved
me
knowing you

Love Songs on a Mixtape

The Sun

You warm me
like stepping into the light of
the sun
after leaving the comfort
of a very cool shade

And for a moment
I enjoy the feel of you
of your touch
adjusting for you
trying to become
as comfortable in you
as I am without you

But standing
in the light of you
hurts my eyes
and burns my skin
a presence that becomes unbearable

So I seek the comfort of the shade
where you light my world
just enough
for the darkness to stay
away

Apart from the Truth

all things apart from the truth
you can't deny
that you wanted me
once, twice,
... more
and that then was not the time
and never was there
a time
that you felt it more
than now
all things apart from the truth
you can't deny
that you want me
now
and that even if now is not the time
never will there be
a time
that you feel it more
than now

Shadows of the Same Soul

You and I
we are like one
shadows of the same soul.
Mirrored metaphors of
enchanting,
soul stimulating memories
like fresh morning mists
after a night's rain.

What you feel,
my heart also touches
What you say,
my soul also speaks.
What you desire
my love also wants.
Through you
I experience myself.
I am myself
as I wish to be felt.
We are like one,
You and I
Shadow of the same soul.

Soft and Fiery

I have been delicate and soft
and delicious and fiery
and precious and wild
sweet like hot caramel melting
in your arms and in your heart
in your hands
You know me as no other
feeling and filling
the delicate softness
and the fiery heat
driving me wild in ways
that have never known enough
pleasure
in each moment
we collide soft and fiery
delicious and wild
in movements shared
between arms and hearts
and hands and mouths
and we melt like
hot caramel into
onto
each other

smile

the skin on my neck
the skin around my navel
my cheeks
i am as succulent
as a berry ripened by the
summer rain.

the pads of my feet
the skin on my lower back
my lips
i am as delicate
as a berry ripened in the
summer sun.

and inside all that
sweetness and
softness
is a fire so hot
i make steam when i
smile

Joy

As my heart beats fast
and my breathing speeds, my mind
sees colors make love.

Remembering Song

I still remember your voice
soft and warm in my ear
and the song that you sang
and the words that
just never made sense
until now
that melodic sweet music
that opens flowers like sunlight
arias
close petals like moonlight
lullabies
and holds me lingering
until the last measure
feeling your music cover me
like rain showers on
blooms
singing your song in harmony
until I can't remember
the words
that now make
sense
because I'm too busy
forgetting myself

Opia

We make love
and eye contact
so intense
the breath of you passes through me
in climatic phrases
and I exhale the
memories of you
back into the atmosphere

I admire your
looks
the looking at me
that unnerves me
and finds me naked and vulnerable
in only a way
that you can
see

She Sings

She sings of many things
of Monday mornings
and Friday flings
Of sunlight kisses
and moonlight tears
of toeing the line
and facing fears
she sings of many things
but mostly
of the pleasure
it brings

Second Thoughts

I am having second thoughts
second thoughts about
how beautiful it feels to be with you
I slip into these thoughts from
time to time
and dream
of seconds
and second chances
but the reality
of the first time's
failure just ceases rotting away
and the stench of that corpse
settles me quickly
no more seconds when there are so many
more
firsts

Love Songs on a Mixtape

Letters to our Daughters

Dear girls,

You are more beautiful and precious than
life and words give purpose or
ways to express

You are more than smiles
and thoughts
and body
and form

You are worlds in yourself
mountains and valleys
formed before
creation
live in you

and whether you birth
mother
or raise another daughter
there will always be girls looking
to you

seeing your greatness
seeing your struggles meld into greatness
because you are more powerful and
stronger than
life and words give purpose

Love Songs on a Mixtape

or ways to express

You are more than
one
you are one of many
in a tribe of strong sisters

Flirt

The door opened
she walked in like a mellow summer
breeze
gently flowing
through an open window.
he stood reading his paper
waiting for his coffee
turning to leave
he smiled a flicker of radiance
like sunlight in morning dew
and her thoughts became
his daydream
and she felt exposed
by the richness of dark chocolate
eyes
full of mischief
And that stride,
that syrupy stride as smooth
as warm honey,
full of confidence
As she ordered her coffee
robust and black smiling a little
at the thoughts
exposed

Dewdrops

Your love's sweet dewdrop
linger on pleasure's petal
ling after our noon

Langston Hughes

Sweet lyrical dreamer
inspire dreams in me
as I collect words
and stack them like
mosaic tiles
against the walls of my mind.
Dreamer of words like
mix matched bits of
randomness
that speaks clearly to
the person that I am.
Dreaming of picturesque words
the dream doesn't fester
like decaying fruit.
Dreaming of agonizing words
my dream isn't deferred
like last-minute worries.
No, sweet lyrical dreamer
inspired by a poet's dream
to be alive
in the imaginative words
that hug me close.
Thanks, sweet lyrical dreamer.
Inspired to a poet's dream
I dream unbridled
as a lover
of words and
I can speak rivers of

Love Songs on a Mixtape

words
that accumulate
like vibrant shards
of shattered tiles
only to be used again.

Moonlight Fingers

Moonlight fingers
through my window
flickering
soft breeze dancing
breathlessly over the sheets
and I think of
how sounds
become words
become languages
become conversations
bodies talk
expressing themselves
me to you
and we
become the words
dancing
breathlessly over the sheets

moonlight fingers
through my window
make me think of you

Wisp

Dandelions wisps
floating freely on soft breaths
spread and touch new loves

Love Songs on a Mixtape

Smell of You

I love the smell of you
earthy,
and salty
just the way a man should
smell on a Saturday afternoon
before the breeze
and after the rain
how nuzzling into your neck
reminds me of all the
times I laughed
at the nonsense
I heard myself say
unaware of how
fleeting our skin
would betray the conversation
and laughter becoming breaths
and breaths becoming
quakes
and the smell of you lingers
earthy
and salty
just the way a man should
feel on my skin

Joy Thief

Pinch the wick
kill the flame
I'm dead behind my eyes
Not a flicker of light
can pass without
darkness stealing
even the smoke from the flame
just like
a joy thief
stealer of happiness
and love

Delicacy

I've been the apricot pit
in a box of peaches
and the only honey in the comb

but I've never
been the apple of your
eye

I've been the crop's
cream
the butter on your
bread

and spilled the milk
that made you cry.

Love is a delicacy
and we aren't on
the menu
or the chef's mind

because I am insatiable and I
can always have a bite.

But what becomes of
this
will be compost

Love Songs on a Mixtape

and we won't remember
our appetites in the morning
because we are so
full at night.

Hold Tight

We shed tears and wipe them away
as we break into
tiny fragments of what we were
in moments shared

with everything lost and our back bent
against
the weight of our nothingness
we find solace
in the likeness
of others
meandering through this same mutilated
dream

we hold hands and hug and shed tears
that exhaust us
for once we feel something
resembling love
for each other
forgetting that in our differences and
isolation

we built castles
in clouds and sand
just as we slipped on the rocks
that should have held us firm

with nothing to lose

Love Songs on a Mixtape

in this world desperately
in need of rebuilding

let us hold tight
to each other our difference attracting
each tiny fragment
creating something
far stronger
than what we once were

Chocolate

The words melt
on my tongue
like chocolate.
I say the things
that I do not mean.
Silky smooth
the words are
as they coat my tongue
in the lies
that come so easily now.
A lavishness developed
by the desire
to harmlessly please
you.
Love's diet isn't just
and the sweet decadence
only lasts briefly
as the chalky aftertaste
of truths untold
melts
on my tongue
like bittersweet
chocolate.

Pizza and Wings

Late night chats
on a quiet stolen night away from it all
conversations that lead to early morning
pillow talk
Laughs over a dinner of pizza and hot
wings
puckering and tingling
sauces staining our fingers
taunting game time cheers
and pleasurable nothingness
as the night stands still
but not really
because tomorrow comes quickly
and we still haven't finished
our late night chats
as the conversations
take us away from everything
to absolutely no where
again
and once again

Love Songs on a Mixtape

Language

Yesterday,
you created a language for me,
poetic
soft sounds
and before my lessons were over
I spoke in whispers softly gesticulating to
you
a conversation unheard,
full of words

Today,
I try to remember you
and the language
rolls around on my tongue
the taste of your words
words, that can't be held forever
but that never fade,
blanketed memories of a conversation
linger
as warm as inside our
conversation

Tomorrow,
I wake knowing
there is no conversation
into the wind I speak for you
remembering the language
in distant echoes

50

Love Songs on a Mixtape

of you
wrapping around me in song
a warmth that holds my heated
monologue
and, baby,
ain't nothing like it

Not Without
Understanding

I am not
without understanding.
I need you to know that.
I begin to speak and you don't
even   hear
                me.

You say, you see me. See, that's
the thing with you visually-aroused-
audio-impotents.
You see me
but you don't hear me.

I'm speaking words so deep and proving
my point so clear
that if this conversation was the Atlantic
Ocean,
I'd be the light shining within the
Mariana Trench
and you'd be
the shadow of a child's
plastic sailboat.

Conversely lacking the stimulation
that I need.

You say that you see me

Love Songs on a Mixtape

and you smile
and I smile
and I pretend that what you say is
intelligent
and funny
and that the sound of your voice
isn't like a hum of a refrigerator.
So that when I speak
you'll listen and not be afraid
of the depth of what I really have to say
I'm not a vision, I'm the visionary.
I'm not a joke, I'm the belly rumbling
laugh

I am all of the thoughts
and expressions
At the bare minimum,
a woman's essence.
So, don't be afraid of what I say
when I answer
what you ask.
You see, I've been
waiting to be heard
to be understood.

Finally

The words
once held hostage
in the private tomes of my soul
finally break free
I am at peace with the world
and the world is at war
with me
Battle bound
unprepared, but fierce
I listen to the cries
and fall prey to
their criticism
and praise
Words escape me
and find solace in the ears,
the mind, and the hearts
of strangers unaware
of the torture endured
as my soul uncontrollably
strips bare
I fret with each
syllable of each
word as the unpaintable
picture of what
I must say
not what I think
becomes a personal masterpiece
and I find peace

Love Songs on a Mixtape

finally
for one silent moment
before I capture
the restless and reckless words
and gently bind them
in my soul
again

The Pursuit

I have discovered that I am
no huntress
Artemis has cursed me for
my Athenian wisdom
and given me the love of
the pursuit
I have discovered that I do not
wish to be captured
bound
tamed
or caged
I want to be free to fly on the wings
of my great hawk
destined for some seclusion
until the next time
I can be hunted again
and again
breathless and giddy
I have discovered that I love
the pursuit.

Secret

I have a secret
I love this feeling that
longing gives me
it is my penance and my redemption
constantly reminding me
inviting me to explore
all the velvety deliciousness
of what could have
should have
would have
been
if the risks weren't measured
and the price wasn't high
so
I keep the secret
loving this feeling

Love Songs on a Mixtape

Nikki

I tried to read some other lady's words
read how she liked summers
and I remembered my
grandmother
baking
and telling stores
at times
I felt her anger at the world
and her need to tell no lies
about the beautiful black men
who shared her thoughts
and desires
and blues
I knew she was a woman
who felt every faction
of her façade
and wore her life proud
high and free

I tried to read some other lady's words
took her book off the shelf
and felt a kindred soul
like sisters
for a while, I couldn't let her go
she taught
me about the beauty
of being a woman
being a poet

Love Songs on a Mixtape

being a lover
and being a Black genius

So when I put her back on the shelf
I left a space for myself

Love Songs on a Mixtape

Earth Shaker, Love Maker

There was never a moment
when the thought of his gaze
didn't send me back in time
to those days
spent outside
in me
on him
on me
the smell of his salty earthiness
as if even Mother Nature
knew that what kept civilization alive
mattered in the scent and feel
of him
a feeling so profound
that even now
imprinted in my mind
are the moments when
the feel of his hands
under my back or
holding my hips
gave me new appreciation for
after thoughts and
aftershocks
because nothing moves
earth like the ways
we meet

Love Songs on a Mixtape

The 25th Hour

Love's finest in the twenty-fifth hour
And all of time stands still
When night and day become like one
and the hearts of lovers revealed.

With endearing words spoken only on a
whisper
And sweet embraces that capture the
soul's breath
True feelings of the heart are given flight
When uninhibitedly we give ourselves.

Love's finest in the twenty-fifth hour
When dreamers meet face to face.
Time knows nothing of a better moment
Than that of the heart's embrace.

These sweetest engagements are sacred
An unmoving moment divinely sublime
Our union is like the sun and horizon
Consummating for an entire lifetime.

Planet to Moon

"one revolution around the sun
and you'll follow me,
my moon"
said the planet
"one revolution by me
and you'll follow the sun,
my planet"
said the moon
dancing about the heavens
elliptical tangoed
waltz
and balance keeps waning
and balance keeps waxing
as the moon dances in shadow
and brilliance
and the planet keeps spinning her along
admiring her
moonlight soft glow

Orange

I peeled an orange today
my fingernail broke through the skin
releasing a fragrant mist
promising sweetness
and as my finger slid between
the hard
and the soft
unable to keep
it together
I thought of you
memories long forgotten
an orange
eaten at my sink
makes me think of you
and before the sweet scent fades from
the soft tips of my fingers
I am hungry
for you
again

Black Man

Thank God and Glory for your
Black beauty,
gentlemen.
Your melanin and his melanin
and definitely their melanin
kissed by the same sun
in the varying degrees of love
made by sunlight and
an open sky
raise that face to mother Sun
so that everyone in nature can see
you are the branches
blooming flowers in a rainbow
of brown beauty
nut-brown and cocoa and chocolate
chestnut and amber and caramel
gold and mocha and tan
ebony and coffee and toffee
burnt umber
and all the shades in between
I am so blessed to
be yours,
Black and beautiful.

Woman

I am aware of my ability to do
as I please and
as you do
as well

and
he may have spoken and
declared that it was your world
and thought that it
needed a woman or a girl,
but all the others never told you
how sweet it sounded when
I whispered the design
into their mind
and
they built me a fleet
and conquered many kingdoms.

You departmentalize in me
what I conceptualize in you
not because you can't see
with your eyes what I feel with my heart
but because you can't feel it,

the essence of what it is meant to be
continued

Love Songs on a Mixtape

A Woman

You fail to acknowledge how
I am
one of the strongest forces known to man.

Creating weakness and havoc
on even the most complex of minds.
I've made
Solomon indecisive,
Sampson a slave,
conquered Rome,
and risen many Trojans
to battle for just the thought of having me

I squatted over valleys and bore
civilizations
I stretched my legs into the sea and you
followed
to new land

without me
your spilled seeds can't plant trees
that will shade Gaia for an eternity
and feed many from my bounty.
But more so than that,
you need me.

When We Lose

Of when times slows to
the moment right before it
feels as if everything moves backwards
so slow that we turn inward on
ourselves and forget
for just one instant
how we can never get it back
the overwhelming pain
and disappointment
like weight gained from
too many celebrations

Of when time moves too fast
and in the stretch of a yawn
todays that should never be
tomorrows are yesterdays
and in the confusion of it
all we forget to remember
to catch our breaths and see
memories grow inside of us
unadmiring and unkempt until we
pluck one

Fire, Honey, Storm, and Flight

I am quick
to express myself
the haste of it feels more passionate
than if I waited a moment longer
impulsivity
negates depravity
and my emotions are of the utmost
importance
so I don't hesitate
when I say that you really
piss me off and

                                  are amazing

make me sick and

                                  complete me

have no idea and

                                  know me so

well
should leave me be and

                                  need to hold me

words uttered so quickly
that they don't require time
because they exist in the moment's feeling
not always perfected by
a second thought
and I am not perfect either
I am the juxtaposition of fire,

Love Songs on a Mixtape

honey,
storm,
and flight
and I don't always know how I am, or
what I am, or where I may land
from the journeys that I take
but I love you within
and without the error of my ways
never changing and never the same
I feel the words as they breeze around me
and through me
racing, spinning on the edge of being
unruly, wild, and liberated
and the world feels perfectly tilted
because
I am quick
to express myself
in love

Love Songs on a Mixtape

Kujichagulia

My sisters and brothers,
why are we so lost
so confused
so inherently ignorant?

I fed my mind on a diet
of poetic words
and militant theories
until I became sick and died
a warrior's death.

I fed my mind on a diet
of mainstream media
and textbook history
until I became sick and died
a slave's death.

I fed and fed and fed my mind
and still nothing felt like me
lost and confused
and inherently ignorant
of me.
Until

Kujichagulia

I am me defined by my actions
and my words

Love Songs on a Mixtape

I am me named by the generations
of brilliant thinkers and lovers
and creators, and destroyers
but I am also me defined by a society
that has no use of me
unless I entertain
seduce
or follow
My sisters and brothers,
let us not be lost
and confused
or inherently ignorant.

Limits, in Honesty

I once felt
words so strong
that the power of a lie
convinced me to change
my truth
but
then you spoke to me
and shattered the illusion
now I tell myself
nothing
I listen to what you say to me
and pretend that I agree
when instead I wish you'd just
fade back into my soul
in truth, souls don't lie
in truth we don't listen
Honesty is so
limiting,
hindering,
the restraints that rub us raw and
gag our voice
so we lie and pretend that we aren't the
thieves, cheaters, liars, murderers
and we lie that we aren't
prejudice, envious, carnal, spiteful,
ignorant
because if we really acknowledge who we
were

Love Songs on a Mixtape

and spoke what we
thought
we would all be the
exact same wretched monster
saying "let's be better"
because our better-than-yours religion
says we should love
one another
and we limit ourselves
and we tell ourselves lies
in hopes of the believing
becoming the seeing
in this
hateful, selfish world
without
a soul

Fading into Light

I am absolutely
Wonderful,
Fine,
Perfect.
Happy
I am absolutely
All the things you do not
Think that I should be
I am
Free
The darkness leaves
Before my dawn
And I am not fading
Into the light
The darkness is fading
Passing
From me
Time has given me a strength
A powerful
Steelness,
The stillness
A desire to become
More of me
And less of us
And none of you
I am absolutely
Dancing away from the shadow
Song in my head

74

Love Songs on a Mixtape

Song of my heart
Fading into the light
because
I am
Free

Exposed

Hidden in shadows
the thoughts that have sprouted
invisible tentacles
that hold me too close
to the edge
of this
beautiful chasm
Those who see me
don't see it
they see me
dancing wildly
in a broken, jagged line
gyrating and
gesticulating
in the rhythmic
hopes of some attachment
that keeps me from falling
in
Not wanting to be caught
needing to be saved
by strong fingers
intertwined in
mine
No, the touch
would expose a weakness
my need to be held
back
down

Love Songs on a Mixtape

close
the touch
would bare my naked thoughts and
insecurities
the part of me that I hide
needing to be
exposed

Honey Locust

I once wanted you close enough to touch
close enough to intertwine myself
and your heart
and our love

but now I overwhelm myself with tasks
and responsibilities
typical garden variety protective gear,
mimicking nature like
thorns on a honey locust

Still I blossom as needed
so that others can admire the beauty
but not get too close
what beauty?
all I see are thorns
that grow out of a mutual
disrespect
beauty?
tell me more and see
how insecurity is fertile

Our distance comforts me
the silence and unspoken disdain
flows like a breeze through bare branches
and fells the leaves and caresses the thorns

It is easy to say the things

Love Songs on a Mixtape

that we want to feel
a closeness that hopefully sheds away
the fear,
the protective gear
the thorns on a honey locust tree

Breakfast

If breakfast is the most important meal of
the day,
then we must be royalty
the living and dining
worthy of immortalizing
don't overindulge me
when knowing exactly
what I want
has always gotten you
what you want
a quick break
cinnamon bread toasted with just enough
heat to give rhythm to the skin
cream cheese warmed and spread
in ripples from end to end
and honey riding the waves in
slow flows that settle
into delicious pools
and we don't break
fast
we eat
not caring
what falls or what spills or what smears
because we anticipate the pleasure of
seconds

Love Songs on a Mixtape

Bitter

Desire tastes bitter
craving what isn't needed. Still,
I relish the taste.

Love Songs on a Mixtape

This too shall pass

I used to write
all the time
because I loved the feel of
it
the way
words became me
and left me like
breathing
and I needed them
kneaded them
manipulated them
as they rolled themselves
music and masterpiece
on paper
Then, I stopped
feeling the words
time fell away
whatever the reason
I lost my words
I lost my voice
this too shall pass
I want to find them again
and as I search
I want to find myself
written in the language that speaks
beyond words
beyond measure
beyond mortality

Wordless

When I am loveless
I am penless and
inkless
so the parched parchment becomes
a crumpled mass on the floor
no words emit from me
I am as empty
as a Saharan desert flower
bloomless without rain

The words are gone
life has left a
world seen and frozen
in my mind
because I am loveless and
wordless
a crumpled mass on the floor
because from me
the words are gone
and without you
I am empty

Love Songs on a Mixtape

Lovers'

Paths glow on golden
skin, damp with kisses and smiles
lovers' speak, du jour!

Love Songs on a Mixtape

The Real

Welcome back to reality
where escapes are merely dreams
because no one can afford to
live the life they want

where we find ourselves stretched
thin and unattached to any one
and no real desire
to reattach

where we are exhausted from the fact
that we are used up and worn out
pretending to be the umbrella
that protects
one another from the rains
that soak us to the bones
where we heal ourselves because
everyone else is sick
but we dare not touch
for fear of contamination
and connection

welcome back to reality
where filters make us beautiful
and desired
but no one wants to see
the ugly hearts they hide
this reality sucks.

Fire(love)flies

Love blooms as fire flies
freely in the twilight dew
flames blaze then fade

Like Poetry

And so,
he asked
"What do you like?"
And I replied
"What all women like.
Poetry."
"To be touched by a finger stroke so soft
that it feels like your warm breath
upon my damp skin.
To be desired by you so completely
that I give only what I want you to have
until that moment of absolution
and I give you
my all.
To be comforted by your love so strong
that my skipping heartbeats
live in the rhythm of yours.

To take your breath and
stay on your mind
and live in your heart
like poetry."

Love Songs on a Mixtape

We are

Whatever we are
is never enough to let go
invisible strings that bind
us and keep us
are the strongest
and we are love
loved in a way
that he can't
and she can't
and they can't disconnect
but we are whatever
and whatever
we are
we
are
never letting go

Diamond Dusted Dreams

If shooting stars
and moonlight are lovers'
destinations
then Heaven is definitely my fate.
Bliss that tangles
Delight that resonates
Contentment that explodes in
the sweetest
supernova
illuminating
the dusting of diamond-coated
dreams
I lovingly share

in these words
for you

Bittersweet

Heavenly bittersweet
memories cloud my judgement
unrequited love

Love Songs on a Mixtape

Love Songs on a Mixtape

.

ABOUT THE AUTHOR

Emeka Barclay has been writing poetry for many years. She considers writing poetry to be intimate and therapeutic. She currently resides in Huntsville, Alabama.

Made in the USA
Monee, IL
10 June 2022

97815187R00059